WHEEL

Michael O'Neill

WHEEL

2008

Published by Arc Publications
Nanholme Mill, Shaw Wood Road
Todmorden OL14 6DA, UK
www.arcpublications.co.uk

Copyright © Michael O'Neill 2008
Design by Tony Ward
Printed by Biddles Ltd
King's Lynn, UK

978 1904614 79 1 (pbk)
978 1906570 19 4 (hbk)

ACKNOWLEDGEMENTS:

Acknowledgements are due to the editors of the following
publications in which some of these poems have already
appeared: *Cape 3, English, The Faber Book of Twentieth-Century
Italian Poems* (ed. Jamie McKendrick), *The Forward Book of Po-
etry 1993, Keats-Shelley Review, London Magazine, New Poetry
Quarterly, Oxford Magazine, PN Review, La Questione Romantica,
The Reader, Spectator, Summoning the Sea* (ed. Wolfgang
Görtschacher and Glyn Pursglove), *TLS* and *Turner Society
News*.

Cover picture: Study for 'The Wheel of Fortune'
by Edward Burne-Jones. Pencil on paper, dated 1873.
© Lady Lever Art Gallery, National Museums Liverpool

The Publishers acknowledge financial
assistance from ACE Yorkshire

Editor for the UK and Ireland: John W. Clarke

For Posy and Jamie,
Daniel and Melanie

Contents

"We stand on a turning wheel…"

from 'We Cannot Hold onto the World'
by Stephen Spender

Post-Mortem

Later, I pushed my son out through the cold,
braking beside a gale-floored oak whose rings

we started to count. 'It lived, oh, ages'
I guessed, stroking a Siamese hair from my jacket.

The white thread jinked through space.
The vet kept calling her 'he', diagnosed

kidney failure and thought 'he may have sulked
in the cattery and not drunk enough.'

'For Suki, when her comes back from hospital?'
What his brash video terms the 'D word'

was proving hard to… Head in hands,
I memorized MacNeice's lines that start

'Out of proportion? Why, almost certainly',
and heard a silence, kink-tailed, round my ankles.

Making a Will

And once again we must entrust to those
who view us by appointment from their desks
the shape or lack of shape of destined loss,
the terror our politeness masks.

Draft follows proof-read draft until
even our deaths are discourse – not our own
but waiting for us in a well-groomed file;
today, the needful thing is that we sign.

We do and, to a legal nod, soon leave,
scenes of conclusion put on hold
while sunlight hurts us like a chance reprieve,
and we resume the lives that we have willed

away to children whom we buckle up
as if for the first time, who, as we drive,
we know will one day glimpse the inner shape
or lack of shape of what we tried to give.

Dawn

Bird-song at dawn;
dawn, when the migraine ebbs away,

when *through the dense mists Mars burns red,*
when, if a figure stood on the High Bridge,

and a camera trained on him performed
a 360 degrees shot, he and the river

would seem to tilt and spin towards the sky;
dawn, when my son comes down, unpicks the alarm's

green, wakeful code, and plugs in *Goldeneye*,
while, still asleep, I dream of you,

my buried friend, of how, one dawn, we hurried
through twisting streets because you wished

to take communion in the gaunt Cathedral.
In my dream, only I emerge,

as one who returns to his lost road.

Cheverny

An evening after rain...
I wander half way down the road
that leads to the chateau, its tufa facade
a shrouded white beyond an arrowed sign.

I stop, turn my back on that house.
and wait. Wait as I've waited for circa
ninety days and three months since the hour
when the phone broke the news to us.

Wait for the halo of the headlamp first,
then, ages later, for the whine
until, up the long approach, the engine
shows itself, and at last

you'll come into view, helmeted and black,
astride the bike you died on, but alive
now, visor lifted, tossing me a wave
before you surge by, leaving in your wake

only the rush and the sigh of the wind
through branches and a chill
I am unable not to feel,
standing in a road that seems to have no end.

Leaves

for Roy Fuller

This autumn we've been treated,
out on our riverside strolls, to leaves buckling

and fluttering, precariously wind-buoyed, dropping
on top of us or into bushes or under foot,

falling and falling until the air seemed
an available dreamscape flecked with gold.

And now they've fallen and the trees are bare.
'The worms will eat the leaves,' our son intones,

recycling a lesson from his new school,
'then the leaves will grow again.'... When your poem notes

'a lenient December', you console
us unconsolingly for what

you had the nerve to look ahead to, the art
to fetch a strange yet homespun music from.

God Talk

'Can I take my toys to heaven?'
Out of the mouths of babes. 'We'll see.'

'Does God have any friends – like Paul and Graham?'
What has been happening at that nursery school?

What happened to...? 'It's been a long day, Dan.'
Sensing a lack of grip, you fling a stare

that makes me knock my drink back, lift you up.
Entangled somehow with a pirate tale,

Dad's low-down on the Most High follows.
Friends walk the plank. 'God saves them, doesn't he?'

A sect of two, we shape a creed
from gold and angels and the Spanish Main.

Your bricks, strewn round the room, await
ascension into some untoppling structure.

Sunday Morning

Swigging your coffee,
you flick through an old notebook:
half-lines collide with earnest notes to self
and a Venetian gag
('Better to keep your mouth shut and appear stupid
than open it and remove all doubt')…
Outside, Princes Street is sprinkled
with scarved Christmas shoppers…
                                    And it lies
before you, not unlike a far field
under snow, an unfolded flatness
shining and curving towards the horizon…

You want to give it a name –
your 'sense of the past', a 'spot of time' even –
but before you know it, it's in your head,
an underground voice you'd been shutting out:
Why don't you walk towards me, lose yourself
in that dimension always beckoning,
always receding?
                    And the brightness melts,
and the impermeable light of a day
with a date and things to do
takes over, falls on your page
like a censor's stamp
or a grace of sorts.

Adelphi Dreams

In at last, inside that flagged structure,
more liner than hotel, ready to slide
down Lime Street towards the Atlantic...

But the botch of my arrival – the woman
at reception, unconvinced by my claim
to be myself, dispatching

proof-seeking faxes – said, or so I took
it to say, 'You're back in a city
where you don't count and can't belong,

and never will.' Which was fine. Good, too,
to take my flu to bed and not lift up
a book or the phone, to beguile the wait

by tracing the steps that had led,
year by year, from 'home' a few miles away
to a soundproofed room, a room with a desk,

two chairs and a nip of despair... After,
I woke in the small hours, tonsils raw,
gulped at the rain and swallowed hard,

then woke some more and heard the fire-alarm.
The corridor was all tranced unconcern.
Not a soul materialised. Ah well,

I thought, plumping the pillow, if one must
return to ashes, why not here, quick flames
leaping higher than dreams of the sea.

Angel

Soon the Jet d'Eau would hang
its spray-blown steeple over Calvin's city.

I was walking off a sore head
bequeathed by the minibar and last night's

luminous signs beyond the lake,
multinational neon daubing the Alps.

Sent down the road that runs along the quay,
a sparrow was hit by a vehicle

it tried to outspeed; whisked
onto the pavement, it lay at my feet,

an augury... In an hour we were lost.
Trudging towards an ice-pink restaurant

to cadge directions from a waiter,
I was stopped in my grumbling tracks

by the shoreline straighter now,
the lake soothed to this analgesic gleam,

the long curve of the Jura peaks,
and, above all, a plane that floated down

like a steel cloud between water and rock
as though the engines had switched off

and the tons of metal were a vast angel
steadying its wings, preparing for the strange

uprush of warmth, the earth's blithe, stained embrace.

Halifax

Not the motorway turn-off town,
but the sweeping Canadian waterfront,

its landing-stage long enough to hold
two troop-ships end on end in the last War.

In malls, along pedways, the living
are a fantasy of politeness, want to know

how your day is going, and to assure you
you're very welcome. If old-world courtesy

means anything, you're finding it
in this new-world port you begin to see

as a youthful veteran who hides his scars...
A French munitions ship collided

in the Harbour with the *Imo* in 1917;
when the flames spread, *Mont Blanc* blew,

the largest man-made fire before Hiroshima,
an exploding sonic rush of death,

plate-glass carpeting the streets, papers
– a single sheet – headlined 'Halifax in Ruins'.

Bodies retrieved from the *Titanic* rest
in the city's three cemeteries.

After Swiss-Air 111 broke up beyond Peggy's Cove
a submarine-like dredger trudged to that scene...

Today a mist disguises Dartmouth's shore.
You watch the ferry head out, then vanish.

Foghorns offer a shifting clue to space,
how it must hang, muffled, over the bridges.

As the veils lift, your sight is tricked
into thinking a tower block has chosen

to be up and off, to stride across the water,
a giant saviour with, you feel sure, gifts

in each hand and a good thought for the huddled
figures on the pier, who await its coming.

Wheel

His flesh seemed less like flesh than dough or clay
kneaded and re-kneaded; he stumbled towards me

like the undead embodiment
of some straggler on the retreat from Moscow,

like… but none of the 'likes' would do
when, under my nose, he tried to mumble the tale

of himself in a species of delirium,
grimed hands cuddling his bottle…

There's no dodging anyone in this city
with its couple of bridges you have to cross;

despite my sidestep earlier he's here,
singling me out as if he knew that I,

briefcase swollen with books and stuff to mark,
had got off scot-free and must pay…

The wound of his crimson-eyed stare!
Crossing his palm with a jingle of change

heals nothing – just earns me
a tangled mutter, more curse than reprieve,

and the sense of looking out at a field
where a vast, spoked wheel slows, then whirls,

the hangers-on – all of them, any of us –
grinning and grimacing before tumbling off.

Stateless

The S-Bahn sweeps you into streets
plotted with care. 'Couldn't have these in England',

you joke about the just-so cycle lanes.
'Why not?' 'Oh, things are too higgledy-piggledy.'

'Higgledy-piggledy?' Later that evening,
after a beer or three, you all stand in a group,

waiting for leave to cross the road,
though there is not a car in sight.

For morning cake and coffee, Rosa takes you
to Lenbachhaus – Kandinskys ride

their blue, abstracted horses… Schellingstrasse:
Sophie Scholl dropping White Rose pamphlets

from a balcony in a hall
like a Lutheran church: 'We shall not be silent.'

Betrayed to the Gestapo by a caretaker,
she's beheaded with her brother and a friend.

Monuments to generals induce pleasantries:
'The British lose all battles save the last',

your host quoting his father – your reply,
'my boyhood hero was Franz Beckenbauer!'

Misunderstandings, murky clarifications
('I'm absolutely not Bavarian';

'Germans don't think of themselves as "Germans"';
'not properly English, not really Irish');

galleries, churches and squares,
imperial calm in the Hofgarten

(sporadic allusions to *The Waste Land*!);
a chilling place-name on the train-route map;

afternoon in the Englischer Garten
with its not very English nude sun-bathers

and quasi-Italian sky you watch
being redefined by stateless clouds,

before you turn away to your concerns –
emails and texts, TV, a restless night,

dreams of a young blonde in a gold sports-car
purring past ruined buildings lit by flames.

Music in the Mirabell
(after Trakl)
for my father

A fountain chants. Clouds heighten
the high blue... white, gossamer.
Come evening, people wander
through the old garden.

A flight of birds twists in space.
Greyness drapes the statue's marble.
A faun with glazed eyes is troubled
by shadows, which melt through darkness.

A leaf drops from the gnarled tree, rust
curling in through a window.
In the room fire's an anxious glow
that calls up ghost after ghost.

A stranger steps across the threshold.
A dog bounds along mouldering walks.
Your ear, as lamps burn down to wicks,
tunes into night's sonata world.

Norfolk

Sand-martins whirling out of cliffs.
Hay trussed in roly-poly bales.

Stalled windmills. Big skies.
A place for weather-watching's rites, for money

to invest in, rewarding itself
with the obligatory boat and a lawn

that tapers off in search of water, life's
elixir, leisure's mirror… Walsingham

and Cromer: the manufactured shrine with
something – nothingness? – candled at its heart,

the deft resort with one eye on your wallet
and one on the enigma of the sky

that bends above the threatened beach
where if, as they heap and spill, drag and heap,

the waves are trying to communicate –
some maxim, perhaps, concerning survival,

the need to endure, to hope just enough –
you find you're baffled, you can't hear a word.

Guilt

At the grille, I grassed on myself,
owning up to all the sins I could muster –

all but that one, the act
not to be spoken of, the sin against,

if not the Holy Ghost, then any chance
of looking God straight in the eye...

A door closed and a skylight disappeared.
In due course it was out into the world

where everyone has views – relief, at first,
then a dull hurt as the years pass

and the views grow verbose or taciturn,
and you wake in the full-blown dark one night

with the absurdest fear you can't expel,
that never again, not in all eternity,

will you be permitted to genuflect
while the sun flares through the great rose window.

Aura

I pace the Prom and stare for a long time
like someone saying goodbye to something ...

The sandbank's dangerous spit; refinery flares;
the railings where, head over heels in love
while tanks crushed Prague and Lucy sowed

the sky with diamonds, I could have thrown
myself into the Mersey's oil-laved arms;
sunset rusting; planes banking out of Speke.

But the buoys' pulsations only recall
Jay Gatsby's light at the end of the dock
when he sensed it was only a light.

What lured a child towards sleep's underworld
composes now a code of green and red,
denoting where the channel's passable,

where not ... Later, Hale-Bopp burns through the night
like a portent out to avenge
an aura on the wane.

I'd tie to the twists of its streaming tails
these lines that tangle farewell words.

Camp

'Doesn't the name just gross you out?',
drawled the blond figure, strumming his guitar.

Incarnation Camp Incorporated –
Jesus and Dives waltzing hand in hand…

We'd bring 'deracination' to an end
according to the khaki-clad Director.

He made us practise role-play. I felt a fool,
roots dangling, yanked from their reserved soil.

The chaplain's beatific smile outscorched the summer.
Pines hummed with the sound of prayer.

I pleaded a Catholic schooling, slunk
back to the tent. Child-free hours! I'd take to my bunk

and watch exotic beetles climb the canvas
– Robert the Bruce, only I was none the wiser,

unlike Dennis, home from Vietnam, face
leathered, eyes a scary blue. Stoned silences.

Then he'd growl 'Git your rear into gear!'
All he got, she wrote in her last letter,

was jail for peddling dope. 'It'll be Fall there.'
Pages dropped like leaves. The pane grew cloudy with distances.

Images

'You'll have to clean my jumper'
you say our toddler

just pronounced 'as dolefully as Eeyore'.
You dab the messed garment with water,

then loop your styled bob behind each ear
of a face whose curves no brush could capture.

After you've left for work, however,
I look up 'Dante and Beatrice'; you know the picture:

the hand-over-heart, hand-clutching-a-flower
confection we once smiled at in the Walker

before we swapped the gallery for the river,
a fresh wind ravelling your long hair

(will every image of you wither?)…
And now you're home, napping on the sofa.

Next Door

Those locals forced to sell, those well-heeled students:
now the blonde saxophonist has gone.

Roxy Music, Mozart, whatever – all grist
to the mill of her lust for improvement...

'Why can't I write as often as she plays?'
In the story I've just read by Richard Ford

Vic spies Cleo in his neighbours' kitchen;
shortly they sleep together – a mistake:

a woman who could cause you big trouble...
'We lived next door,' you tell our visitor,

then smile at me.
I glimpse you, apparitional, at a window.

The new couple lay down hammer and drill,
their voices fluting from a hollowed room.

Versions

'My father in the "Study", book in hand,
pipe-smoke wreathed above his armchair.'

This for the social worker who requires
two sides about our childhoods please

(part of our application to adopt)…
Is that thin figure circling round a field

a sister or a brother? I delete
'long grass, an orchard, a green world'

in favour of an anecdote or two
I hope will do – then scrawl:

His wife and son were out. He tried once more:
'I had no family. Grew up on my own.

Watched clouds. Wrote stories opening
"My father in the 'Study', book in hand…"'

Idyll

A boy, newly ten or so, springs awake
to gaze at protective trees, dew on the grass
when soon he'll practise his Brian Statham action.

Blossom loiters on a breeze from the Mersey
that throws him off the scent of evidence
starting to impinge: bomb-sites staring back

as the car sped towards the centre,
St Luke's ripped open for the sky's inspection,
what a friend swore his Dad said…

Shut your eyes and leave him
to movement off the seam; don't let him glimpse
how, decades on, he'll walk up the drive

in a trapped dream to find only himself,
a boy bowling, the sole inhabitant
of a fictive idyll – only himself

and a family of ghosts looking on
silently as round goes his arm,
brushing his ear, while colour bleeds

from grass in the wake of his follow-through,
and the cherry trees have the look
of figures who upheld a world.

Fall

He came to a place
where light was all shut out,
and met Francesca da Rimini.

'I only give interviews', she pouted
with a shrug of her glamorous shoulders,
'to you know whom. So,'

– pausing for effect, eyes wide open –
'who the hell are you?' With that,
she turned her lovely, fed-up face

towards the pale dope
who followed her everywhere;
they whirled off through the darkness.

And he fell for her, fell
the way a man falls when
his body falls to its death.

He kept saying to himself:
'I came to a place
where light was all shut out,

fell in love with
Francesca da Rimini,
and no longer heard the cranes,

their slow, migratory chant.'

Waiting

You went downstairs and started reading Dante:
   absence of hope puts on bleak form
   when, walking on a lake which looks like glass,

the pilgrim recognizes, underfoot,
   dolorous spirits wedged in ice,
   a glacial dungeon crammed with those

who turned their wills against their great Creator...
   You waited for the dawn, and for a voice
   like that which held entranced the listeners (to

stern Cato's indignation) as it sang
   (the sweetness resonates within them still)
   'Love that converses with me in my mind'

– you've not stopped waiting for that voice, that dawn.

Void
(after Baudelaire)

Pascal had his void; it went with him.
But the void has the lot – action, desire, dream,
language; and I've known dread,
a breeze lifting my hair from my head.

On each side space, an endless drop,
silence and more space – mesmeric, big with fear.
God the director stages a cracker
of a nightmare; the small hours are the backdrop.

Sleep scares me like a pit
crawling with forms that horrify sight.
The infinite crowds in at every window,

and my mind, seized by vertigo,
wants nothingness, no-feeling.
Christ! never to shrug off numbers and being!

Caught

All day I feel like a man on a quay,
ceasing to wave at a vanishing sail…

If anyone saw, I decide tonight,
you did, circling round in a ring of souls.

Does your gaze catch me fretting, writing
'Years are a mist through which a shape

forms when one mouths "Not much is real; you were"'?
Once, you caught me out when you found

the stalk of an apple under my bed
(the flimsiest stalk – I'd devoured the core),

which put you up there with the great Sherlock;
your frown was the guardian of my sleep…

'She sleeps in the calm earth, and peace is here'
droned round my head while the coffin was lowered,

sedated migraine and the opened grave.
But you're no more in the earth

than you're in the heaven you so deserve.
You're in my head. Sleep in my head.

Lost

After Benediction hot drinks then bed,
the moon rising from the monstrance of a cloud.

*

Venice. Years on. And years ago. We doubled back
and missed our way and came upon a square

shuttered and sun-struck, with a dead-end look.
A pack of stray cats baked.

*

Candles. Candles and worn eyes. And the words:
'Tower of Ivory… Queen of Peace.'

*

Tonight the moon is full, a systematic white;
you're in the dark or at any rate lost,

or caught for ever in that moment by a window,
or on a vaporetto heading for the island of the dead.

*

'Lost', you say, liking the sound. Also 'candles',
'years', 'Venice', 'monstrance'. And then again 'lost'.

Crush

'Our Lady?' asks my son, almost seven,
thrown, to my causeless surprise, by the title.
He's heard of God and Santa Claus and heaven,

but not of her I'd worship on my knees
as a boy in the tucked-away side-chapel,
having risen early to serve Low Mass.

Private devotions! Mary, I've not been
able, it seems, to abjure, develop
or transmit the crush I had on

you; fluted, plaster blues adorned my room,
holding spirits at bay all night,
the erotic-sacred backdrop to each dream,

part of a past I've left behind and move
towards... 'You know, Jesus's mother,' I say,
'whose kindness you can always be sure of',

my voice sliding into a reverie
of sashed processions, benedictions, the black
Madonna in the Dordogne to whom we

prayed for a child at a difficult time.

Going Back

I go back seldom now and all the time;
it's twilight and I'm playing with my brother;
the sound I hear's the rush of limbs and breath
and years… I am myself and someone other.

Beyond our games the Long Room gleams
into the bonding darkness; figures roam
about the house and into their own lives.
I gesture at the pane, then drop my arm.

I go back seldom now yet all the time
it seems as though an atmosphere at dusk,
through which I strain to score a goal and find
the air's composed of links I risk

tearing apart, enmeshes me.
Night seeps from wardrobes; voices tread the stair.
The buoy's red signal sends me off to sleep,
to a strange place I know and need and fear.

Looking On

You isolate, as in a still,
the fall-out of his misfired joke, her eyes...

You should have intervened, and yet
the earth won't shatter, will it? There's

a loss of balance in letting yourself
be reminded of a school disturbance:

the lads half unscrewing the legs
of the library desk where they'd decreed

the boy labelled 'bent as a nine-pound note'
– he'd kissed a friend, and not just once,

so hot-faced rumour raged – should sit.
It wobbled sideways, then crashed to the floor

when he pressed muffs of flesh against his ears
to shut out taunts. Satisfied grins...

Closing your textbook made a snapping sound.
Light settled on a wall-map of the world.

Bengal Night

Pertly, a petrifying dream, she glides beside me.
Seven or so. 'Foreign currency?
American dollar? English pound?' 'Controlled by goons',
I'm assured later. In the pre-dawn heat,

I've emerged luggageless from Kolkata airport
where a man who speaks no English holds a sign,
then whisks me away till the girl stops beseeching.
His friend drives, foot right down.

Bouncing off the car, a stray dog
emits a cry of shocked, blood-freezing pain
and is lost amidst the potholes as on we batter
past small fires, crouched forms and shells of houses I beg

whatever god presides here at night not to allow
people to live in. Soon we roar down emptied Park Street,
take a left and blast the horn...
                          The gate
opens, allotting me my room, the gang

of strident crows sweeping from roof to tree,
the silence and the service, and the Raj
seeping its ghosts from portraits and from shy
motions of the head throughout the Club,

while out there, night after night, a girl,
long since vanished from the wing-mirror,
mimics with angelic pitch the mumble
of one more visitor's appalled rejection.

Non-Combatant

You come back late and listen to
a CNN reporter, mike extended
through a window, wafting the sounds of war
into the shelter of your living-room:

alliterative bombs or 'Triple A'
which hold you paralysed though free to check,
before going to bed, that bit from Swift
about spectators and their 'great diversion'.

Lines

Rain doodles come together and diverge
like railway-lines or lines

that keep forgetting how to rhyme, or like
windows in the organ factory opposite

at one of which I've glanced since lunch,
hoping the sight of the man with a saw

and a job to complete will spur
me on to hold in words whatever it was

that sent a dream packing in the small hours
and lifted the roof off the room I slept

in as a child, which was changed now, what with
the music, though just the same, just a bed

and a life, and the effect was pure *Twin Peaks*,
plangent and aching and pointless and null.

Dream Families

You seemed older, other, drumming your feet,
staring at workmen, the ghost of your face.

The waitress brought our beans and stuff,
prize for the trip to court where we'd applied

to adopt the baby – your sister
unless the girl who bore her claims her back.

The drilling vanished. You toyed with a chip.
Ours had the briefest air of the stray bondings

I'd been drawn to for weeks in films by Wenders
– dream families that never were rehoused

in lonely minds… Perhaps a jet
ploughs past the window of some void hotel

where the man smokes, gazing without a smile
at the shrewd, defenceless, faraway sleeper.

Adoption Hearing

A smoker would have scorched through packets. *Should
we lose her, I would think of here as cursed.*

'Just a formality' – then why had the ass
debarred us from his presence for three hours

when all we wanted was his rubber stamp?
The harassed clerk appeared and disappeared.

We'd gone away and fed you and returned,
the last case to be heard. Elsewhere, judged lives

knew shock or certainty or, as with us
after those wheezy mutterings, relief

glimpsing beyond itself a day like this
rinsed by the kind of light that comes off snow,

while you, wispy princess in your highchair,
wave the splodged sceptre of a spoon.

Spell

'Have you had a long day?',
   she asks.
Between the squalls such tenderness and care!
   Worlds lie all before her,

which makes me hold my breath.
   What does she know
save what she learns, and what have I to teach
   who learn from her that much

of what I think I know
   is wasted time?
She comes back, weeping and complaining, down
   on her luck, a fraught moan

bent on redress; cheered up,
   she studies these
green symbols forming as the cursor moves,
   reducing to 'Dad loves

his small-boned, large-eyed daughter'
   – breathed like a spell
to ward off spirits of the night that find
   work at the long day's end.

Appearances

'Appearances', he snorts,
and who can blame him. You sift through days –
so busy, so important, so unreal;
only the oddest rag of circumstance

still eddies in the memory.
The solace is that little stays
to haunt or to reproach, except the lack of things
to haunt or to reproach... Appearances,

appearances – your daughter, fifteen,
stowed in the back seat, in a spiked haze.
Now that upset you and you kept vigil
beside her bed; waking her twice an hour
to help her navigate the druggy maze,
you prayed appearances would be resumed.

Exchange Visit

Low-spirited, high-cheekboned, pale,
he gestured, 'There, it is not possible',
then the sheaf was handed over
with a shy, clandestine air:

poems written to 'improve' his English.
Most flamed with desire, anguish,
angels and demons, hell or paradise.
The best I told him was a quieter piece,

homesick for snow, buildings, his family.
Years had made him more trace than memory
until the revolution
melted winter and faces shone.

All week his forward-toppling script
crossed my field of vision. I kept
seeming to read - in the street, in bed, wherever -
'You were wrong, you were blind, reconsider.'

Hope

Hope, that anchor trailing through space,
that long deferred doth make the something sick,
that hollows you out like an illness.

Hope – there's not a week
when you don't meet one another casually,
have a brief chat, change tack,

and wander off, back towards the fleecy
clouds you sometimes glimpse still hanging on
just as twilight wants to speak a little darkly…

Hope: that travelling torch, game companion
who, when the cold bites, ventures the view
that you can be too much in the sun,

who, neck in sand, will have nothing to do
with sulks, and has only good in mind for you.

Stare

Hardened baby faces
lean towards fields and lived-in spaces

their rockets are colouring swiftly,
visiting apocalypse upon Charlie.

Then I was slightly more callow.
The moon, some nights, filled the attic window

as though carved from ice; cranes
lit up and blocked my hunt for signs

while 'Heartbreak Hotel' spilled into the room,
its rooms a dismal, glamorous honeycomb.

Verbs would be memorized, terms would vanish
along with Speech Days, their pomp and tosh.

But what of the feeling of free fall
so unlike Satan's epic tumble?

Out there was a system or a chaos; how
to tell the difference? And who,

if not one of the victims, is this Marine,
face bruised and hollowed, clutching his weapon

like a comforter, captured on TV,
his drugged gaze staring beyond me?

There

'There is this other place. It's where we live
although we are forbidden to go there.'

For days the phrases hound his walks, confront
him in the mirror, wave across the bar

to where he sits with his glass of red wine
– phrases which mock their trust like arms extended

towards a fake shore. And yet he swigs back the hope
that dreams will map co-ordinates of a place

breathing a stillness so like movement
he might not be dreaming but stepping

out of a house only to enter its double,
except that where the first house now looks dark

the second glimmers – on the front door letters
beckon; he reads 'There is this other place...'...

Corridor

   Put it this way... Long rain
patterns the windows of a cluttered room
   where shadows hug a man
who looks out at roofs, shrugging off a dream –

   a dream in which he traipsed
through a ploughed landscape on a wintry hike,
   hearing himself say 'lapsed,
elapsed', suspecting there was no way back –

   when suddenly wet veils
tore and he saw it again (this time fire-
   vaulted, with air for walls,
and paced by bodiless shapes), the corridor

   running beyond the start
and forwards to an ending which appeared
   to be no ending but
the first note of a song he'd never heard.

Turneresque

'He has been here,
and fired a gun',
said his crest-fallen
rival, whose *Opening
of Waterloo Bridge*,
all liquid tints and high sheen,
appeared to have met
its own Waterloo
after the high-coloured,
squat fellow had blown
in and left his mark
bang in the foreground
of the next-door oil,
a burnt-coal
red addition
to the craftily
subdued marine
greys, a 'round daub'
just bigger than
a shilling coin,
which later he'd glaze,
with minutes to spare,
shaping a buoy
that set its now
scarlet seal
on the paint as
it rode the swell.

The Half-Landing

Pausing on the stairs, you see
    through the window at the half-landing
that the sky is now a stoic
    blue the shade of a bruise.

A bruised heaven, drawing your eye
    upwards in a self-mocking
arc of transcendence…
    Cloudily, unmistakably,

something about you drops away
    like a sack carried for so long
you'd forgotten how heavy it was.

You tilt, as though from purgatory,
    towards a dream of release, until
the next stair brings back roofs, dwellings.

Unspoken

You wanted no one to know,
    which is fair enough and why
I sit here imagining things
    I'd have said at your bedside,

such as *We had the same grandparents.*
    Remember the back lane that ran
from the vicarage to the village green?
    Perhaps you were too young...

Hardly a word we shared
    comes back and yet your smile slips
in and out of my days

    like a vapour trail
stretched with unbearable
    slowness across a tall, cold sky.

The Line-Manager's Soliloquy

Too many nights pacing
the floor of your skull, trying not
to trip over the furniture
of angst; too many nights.

Too many evenings writing reports,
too many days entangled
in the net of the will of others;
too many days and evenings.

Too many hours hearing wheels turn
within wheels, even as you long
for them to grind to a gradual,
silent halt; too many hours.

Too many times spent outwitting
the strategies of someone
else's ego, until that ego seems,
too many times, to be your own.

Too many meetings at which you've
ruled in favour of a course
of action for… what? the common
good? Certainly, too many meetings.

Too many friendships lost, too
many acquaintances made, too many
months you've slogged on, despite
saying over and over, 'Too many…'.

Moments

Keith Douglas found in killing a knack or a skill,
a damnable grace that sent grace packing:

dial steadied, finger tensed, the human
at an inhuman depth of concentration,

state entered by sniper, lyric poet, and these –
throwers of hammer, discus, and the rest.

Their end the accomplishment of an action,
their actions belong, like those of sniper or poet,

to no one's republic, despite waved flags,
and dream of transcending themselves

as though they took their inspiration
not from sweat, rivalry, hatred, or need

but from some aesthete's sub-Platonic heaven
where perfection or its simulacrum

narrows cold eyes and offers to consume
its worshippers in unrepeatable moments…

Bounding steps, dragged stride, the do-or-die grunt:
in the 'city of bombs' which in '36

sought to stage a 'People's Olympiad',
a city which suffered, and fought with itself,

and was bombed, and fought on, and lost –
in this city a javelin, say, arcs upwards

against flash-bulbs imploding round the stadium,
draws history, for a second, into its wake,

levels out, shaft buoyed by resistant air,
then wounds the turf and shivers, the brief quest over,

the world record unbreached or breached, the world
breaking in like a Colosseum roar,

the lips letting out an intake of breath,
the tracksuit slipped back on like a wry knowledge.

It

It hangs around, above… a mist that drifts
across the windows of tall buildings –
the air you breathe out and inhale,
a shout across Republic Square, the lifts
announcing themselves with a bump at each landing
inside some package-holiday hotel
where locals endure the onrush
of tourists with their needs and cash.

Or it can be as, once, when, for a week,
you woke up to the reign of the Twin Towers
scaling the heavens. You craned your neck,
but could hardly, from your slightly swaying floor,
project your sight to summits those crazed fires
would melt and topple days after your departure.

Popeye Village

'Boys and Girls, Boys and Girls!
Our next show is called the Puppet Show
and this show will be held at the School House
in about five minutes time. See you soon!'

Familial, newly old, I sprawl
in the Beaver Sawmill like a forgotten extra,
gazing beyond a cliff in Anchor Bay
at the first sweep of the Mediterranean.

Phoenicians plied their trade, unloaded wares
at harbours round this sea; today,
the tinted coaches bulk against the sky,
while Olive Oyl and Popeye squabble
behind me, and light seduces water
as if to lure me on, or leave me stranded.

Daypex

1

Your Daypex ticket has imprisoned you
in this cathedral city all day long.

Those literary folk have stood you up;
no go-betweens in the L. P. Hartley Room.

Still, now you've trodden the aisle
where Katharine of Aragon rests.

She paid the price for being 'simplex'.
You kill time in a bar, then watch

the merry-go-round in Cathedral Square,
horse after horse melting into a whirled

hoop of light. Vendors of Santa hats
brave the hours you count down, until

you fetch up on the platform as a train,
the one before your chariot of release,

awaits its coffee-seeking driver and
you gaze at a girl's tensed profile

before the driver climbs aboard, the whistle summons,
and the stage of the train departs,

conveying such lit scenery
as clarifies the bleakness of the night.

   2

This in your head, and then the email
telling you the organiser

was absent, and the event cancelled,
because (but the letters began to jumble),

because of a suicide (but all you'd done
was *kill time*) the previous day.

The ticket lingered on
in the ward of your wallet for months;

it rebuked you somehow, pricking your skin
when your fingers revolved its edges

and it turned itself, once more, into lines.

Probably Not

Scent of wild garlic
borne on the June rain...
You cross
the award-winning bridge
(gaps between slabs)
head full of Plath,
how she simply
could not see where
there was to get to,
and of words you wrote
once: 'Cow-parsley
glimmers - snow of June'.
That poem didn't live;
it's a sad diagnosis.
Can a man understand...?
Probably not,
but you'll bring
to your lecture
sympathy with failure
and mishap:
so hated by Plath,
princess of waxy perfection,
that they compose
a foe her poems
are bent on slaying,
a foe hand in glove
with fate,
with the fixed stars:
failure and mishap,

which broke into a grin
last Saturday night
when a police car
hove into view,
blue lights whirling,
before you were questioned
– 'That'd be a full
bottle, would it, sir?' –
then breathalysed
for a dread
few minutes,
during which
you slid into
this other life
where ruin was
your new best friend.
 'Deep breath, please;
then exhale slowly…
I like to wait
a full twenty seconds.'
But the light
stayed a glorious,
inculpable green
reflected on the cupped
palm of the Law.
'Not a trace of alcohol'
– said with a shade,
with the faintest tang,
of disappointment.

Allowed to exit
('my colleague will now
release the lock'),
you walked back to your car,
and opened the door
that readmitted
you to the world
of opulent drabness
and lack of event,
where you might, with luck,
survive the while.

Gloss

i.m. Alan Ross

Someone's uncorrected proof copy
sent for my next piece – howlers
caught by an in-house hand or missed…

Inside, you'd sketched an elegy
for Joseph Brodsky; it recalled
smoke-haloed talk

in a restaurant, possibly the place
you took me to the times
I found my way to your South Kensington

office, the shed with books piled high,
which you'd urge me to bear off,
a diffident looter – 'don't feel you have

to read them, but if any should appeal…'.
I wish I could unearth, from the shambolic
chaos of my shelves and papers, that copy;

below the find of your quatrains
I'd scrawl my gloss on their author:
clipped, unpompous speech, gossipy wit,

and forthright judgement ('too much cleverness
in poetry today – give me
one good lyric by Spender, something that comes

out of deep feeling'): these were yours;
also kindness that never flinched
from pointing out a bad line, or from ringing

weeks before your death, your beautiful voice
poised as ever, to say, 'I've been a bit mad,
but I'm fine now – would you like to review…?'

Dawn
(after Cardarelli)

Only in you, dawn, is there ease
for the laboured breathing
of the death I bear with me.
Only in you is there a cure
for my insomnia, which resembles
a thunderous river,
plundering, infernal,
where, each night, I descend,
battling in vain...
That's when you appear,
always arriving so stealthily
you almost frighten,
and eavesdrop and spy,
most vagabond of ghosts,
white-faced dawn.
The nightmares stop,
the phantoms vanish.
Death, my gloomy
companion through the small hours,
leaves, sloping off
with the tread of a thief.
I emerge from it all
and retrieve myself
out of the dark currents;
shaken, I take refuge
in a petrified sleep.
– Dawn, charitable dawn,
sea of uncertain light,
in which everything finds a source.

Bypass

The skyline looked brand new
that visit. The three Graces, Albert Dock,
and the Cathedrals – all of them looked brand new.

It was as if the wave of pride
at the announcement that the city
would be the next capital of culture

had risen up, grown literal,
and drenched ambitious stones.
I'd already found a second-hand bookshop

(auspicious sign), run by a man
who talked about Iraq,
the sort of person I went to school with,

who'd tell me what to read
as we wound back home on the 60 bus.
You'd be in your Consultant's suit,

cursing the day's out-patient list...
I'd have made a story of this for you,
but my heart wasn't in it, too worried

by yours, due to be quadruply bypassed
in a few days. We strolled on; stopped;
you dwelt on the river with a changed look,

quoted some Latin in a fluent voice,
one of your scholastic maxims
(Jacques Maritain to the rescue!),

and joked about the folly
of racing to the top of the St Ives Tate,
'though why they place the café where they do...'.

Massive structures of stone
rose behind us, while we took in the light
and watched the ferry leave the landing-stage.

Venetian Triptych

I SEPTEMBER
(after Cardarelli)

Already – it's only September –
Venice plays host
to a carnival of ghostly shiftings;
its stones are draped in shadow.
The sun's last ray falls
on gold mosaics and burns
them like straw: a dazzling sight.
Meanwhile, behind the Procuratie,
the moon rises like magic.
Festive lights with a silver sheen
float distantly
through the cold, turning air.
I look on, bewitched…
Later, perhaps, I'll remember
some of these fine evenings
which are quick to come and go.
Then the lights
will seem more brilliant, more alive,
and though they made me despair a little
(always beyond me, always elusive!),
they will blaze within me, then,
so many stars in the mind's sky.
At that point, I'll know content of a sort,
a shaped calm.

II Precious Little

That afternoon we failed to go to Venice
felt like a missed chance multiplied until
all chances vanished with it. Not for us,
a criss-cross circuit of the Grand Canal,

or San Michele with its cypresses,
or inlaid gold, or moving out of shadow
into glare on leaving Ca' Rezzonico…
We dozed, heat-stricken, through the breaking news.

Yet when we surfaced from that capsuled cabin,
the upper air was all the fresher. Rain
and sun had signed a treaty, while a breeze
flicked off the water like a sidling voice
with precious little to provoke us with except
'Good that you've woken, better that you slept'.

III CALCULUS

Shorelights flared and vanished. The boat bore on
to Jesolo, marshes drained by the Boss
before the hotels mushroomed – ten miles of them –
after the War. One for the calculus!

Not everything ends in loss – or does it?
Crossing the lagoon meant 'lagoon'
had yielded up the sense of something dark
and changeable, yet stored when gone.

So, why not start again? *The boat bore on.*
The unimaginable city lay astern.
Beams from the cabin sparkled
in zigzag lines across the water. Engines

pulsed…
            and I almost said out loud, 'it's as
though where we are is never quite the point,
as though shorelights will continue to blaze,
even when journeys eclipse them.'

Spinners

Spring warmth in the midst of late snow:
you take it in as though it were,

if not the last, then one
in a sequence that is diminishing…

Last night you chewed a pencil
over your daughter's homework:

the crooked laws of probability.
If three friends spin three spinners and each spinner

has five sides and each side is a new colour…
Today, the walk to work's an allegory

as you climb past the river up the path
that leads to the Cathedral you don't enter,

murmuring your own equations:
one day becomes another, one decade

*forgets the last, one life seems not to have
happened.* Not much of an answer, but

the chopper's whirring voice above the Prison
has it sussed: *even if each*

*spinner stopped spinning at a different hour,
there'd be one end only to their spinning.*

Infinity
(after Leopardi)

It's always been dear to me, this hill
and this hedge that almost hides
the farthest horizon.
Sitting and wondering, though, I conjure up
void spaces beyond them
and more than human silences
– unplumbable quiet in which my heart
half-frightens itself. And hearing the wind
gust through this windbreak, I compare
infinite silence
with the wind's voice; and what haunts me
is the eternal,
and the dead seasons, and the present season,
its life, and the sound of it. In this fashion,
the mind drowns in immensity;
and it's good to be lost in such a sea.

Compass Needle

Beside a tendon a blue vein
winds under the skin of the hand

with which you scribble a postcard
then fiddle with the catch of a new bracelet.

It's less that it has a life of its own,
your tanned, long-fingered hand,

than that it channels the flow of your life
on this boneshaker to Valletta,

in which we bounce along with passengers
who bless themselves – we can see why – when boarding.

Or it's less that it channels your life's flow
than that it... whatever the cause

I'm drawn to you, for the umpteenth time,
like a compass needle tugged to the north.

Blue

At 30,000 feet, the breathed-in present;
tenacious engines drive us on.
The blue above the stilled horizon line
recalls an emptied tomb, forsaken tent,

seems absolute.
                      A question you relayed
once – *Who can know we count for anything?* –
issues out of the drone like a wry song,
a kind of affirmation now you're dead.

For 'gone from us as though you never were'
– I couldn't say that, even if the blue
enigma served as slender proof that new
dwellings received you now, smiling, eyes clear.

Toys for the Boys

The wheel of fortune is the merest toy
if viewed from the perspective of the gods,
or so it seemed when each was just a boy.

'All strategies of power are but a ploy',
the first avows, and grins. 'For most poor sods,'
he adds, 'history's wheel spins like a toy.'

Fortuna's slender figure and her coy
refusals turn into whips and vicious rods
– that's how a second thinks when not a boy.

'Her smile', he rages, 'serves only to annoy;
she thrives on cross-purposes, on being at odds,
lashing her wheel like a malicious toy.'

In middle age a third learns the harsh joy
of seeking to be one who plods
and does not try to run as when a boy.

That way, he reckons, no one can destroy
what's not yet made… But, to the end, some force prods
and taunts them with 'Although this wheel's a toy,
you're bound to it, each of you, man and boy.'

Biographical note

MICHAEL O'NEILL was born in Aldershot in 1953, and in 1960 moved to Liverpool. He read English at Exeter College, Oxford. Since 1979 he has lectured at Durham University, where he is a Professor of English. He co-founded and co-edited *Poetry Durham* from 1982 to 1994. His critical studies include *The All-Sustaining Air* (OUP, 2007), an exploration of Romantic poetry's influence on poets since 1900.

He received an Eric Gregory Award in 1983 for his poetry and a Cholmondeley Award for Poets in 1990. His collection *The Stripped Bed* was published by Collins Harvill in 1990.

He is married and has two children.

Recent titles in Arc Publications'
POETRY FROM THE UK / IRELAND

LIZ ALMOND
The Shut Drawer

JONATHAN ASSER
Outside The All Stars

DONALD ATKINSON
In Waterlight: Poems New, Selected & Revised

JOANNA BOULTER
24 Preludes and Fugues on Dmitri Shostakovich

THOMAS A CLARK
The Path to the Sea

TONY CURTIS
What Darkness Covers
The Well in the Rain

JULIA DARLING
Sudden Collapses in Public Places
Apology for Absence

KATHERINE GALLAGHER
Circus-Apprentice

CHRISSIE GITTINS
Armature

MICHAEL HASLAM
The Music Laid Her Songs in Language
A Sinner Saved by Grace

JOEL LANE
Trouble in the Heartland

TARIQ LATIF
The Punjabi Weddings

HERBERT LOMAS
The Vale of Todmorden

PETE MORGAN
August Light